When Stuff

Is Not

Enough

Michael G. West

When Stuff Is Not Enough
Sepiessa Press
64 Madaline Lane
Vineyard Haven, MA 02568

ISBN-13: 978-1518705595
ISBN-10: 1518705596

DEDICATION

For someone I haven't yet met

Enough?

So many celebrations, so much expressive music, dancing and drinking, so many entertaining plays, eye-beguiling movies, so much art, poetry, ballet, opera.

I sit meditating when I'm not reading or writing. Or I'm feeding, walking, playing with my dog.

That -- and family -- fills my time to bursting.

Still I yearn. Why? Isn't this simple life enough?

Who and what more could I let in?

Or, rather, what should I let out?

After Kido

On this cold night the bamboos stir,

Their sound -- now harsh, now soft --

Steals through the lattice window.

They say the ear is no match for mind,

I say who in flickering lamplight

Needs a single scripture leaf?

After Kokuin

I'm sixty-seven years old

And sometimes sought the Way

Just this morning we passed

Like strangers on the road

After Wang Wei

These days I love only silence --

The things of this world are no more.

Looking back, I know no better way

Than this, returning to the grove

Where pine breezes lift my robe,

Moonbeams play across my lute strings.

What, you ask, is the ultimate truth?

Out on the lake a fisherman is singing.

After Yangshan

Please don't force your mind

Down the rocky path

Of these teachings,

As you may stumble needlessly.

Just turn toward the deep

Ocean within you,

Know its tides, the waves

Crashing upon the beach.

Vérité

Caught in bare branches

Of a scrub oak one lone maple leaf

Shivering in the wind

A lover taking refuge

In the arms of another

The setting sun reflecting

In a side view mirror

Of a car parked far from home

Marriage

What a sexy beast you be

Like monkey climbing

Puzzle tree

Once high above

You looking round

No way to get down

Ouch!

Sharp spines

All pointing up

Easy climbing one way --

Getting down?

Not so much.

Just This

Nothing is forever not even diamonds

Dripping blood

Of the mine workers who've struggled

Since time began to feed their children

Not soaring mountains

Their high peaks barren of snow and bird cries

Not endless ocean waves rippling to distant horizons

Not uncountable miles of desert

Sand grains swirling in the wind

Not how I feel about you

Not how much time we have

Together now

Just this moment

Just these few words to share

Just this: silence

Pretty Lies

If all the best lies have the most truth

As you claim, fingers crossed

I want the one with the highest proof

Like Everclear 190 or maybe

Moonshine distilled from eternal wisdom

Not some fortune cookie

Stuffed with half-truths and rumors

I want Snopes to verify

So I can believe

When I look into your eyes

Pull your body close to mine and taste

The breath you've shaped into such pretty lies

Rendezvous: Mangled Draft

I been lyin'

Here since the Mesozoic

Mama

Come closer so I can cuddle your bones

That's the way

We keep our selves

From turning to dust and smudges

The smell of hunger in your blood

The taste of salt in the crook of your arm

18

The look of surprise when I dive down

The heat from your furnace

The roundness of your moaning

When afterward

We have nothing to say but savor silence

I know with the certainty that death awaits

One day you will be gone from me

Nothing green but crumbles

The pain that dances in my eyes and mind

Like static pops on a 78

Will be mine again

And such joy as seemed endlessly eternally real

Will sit alone in a darkened theater

You are my visitor and only for this moment

Can we push from our lives

The reptilian dread of shadows

We ourselves cast upon the face of a child

Except when the sun at its zenith

Burns through the conservatory glass

Or fair skin singed by godless Helios

Gone to Hades to shine upon the dead

Cries out for darkness

For there is no justice only fate

And you and I can only seize

Little forbidden pleasures that have tempted us

We can only touch what we mustn't

Muss what is orderly and fussed over

Dance against the beat and sing off key

Lie when commanded to testify

And bite what we should lick with our tongues

Else like the meekest lamb shorn of its curls

Slaughtered for chops

Whose bleating cries faded and unheard

Leave not a trace

We vanish from our own minds

With the love we made

Blood and cum and spit and sweat

Sheets torn and pillows tossed

Shirts stained, earrings lost

In unfamiliar unmade beds rented by the hour

Haiku

Mandalas of colored sand

design to be

undone

Sequence

Sky drips

cold sweat

trees last leaves

Ancient words

dancing

rhythm in the rain

Blue pearl

beyond price

soaring through space

Days of rain

wet leaves

new sun

Terrible

we dream of things

that never are

Bare oak branches

one elm leaf

seeking asylum

Everything stops

birds, rabbits frozen

blue shadow

What Have We Done?

Sequence in Variation on a Basho haiku

1

Lotus pond

a frog jumps in

plop!

2

Dying lotus pond

one-legged frog leaps

splop! ripples

3

Pond thick with muck

no flying bugs, no frogs

lingering stink

Two Deer Haiku

Deer darts through headlights

instantly, almost unseen

rubber on asphalt

Another shoots past

missed him? how?

dumb luck or omen, breathe

Island Winter

Mind drops away in snowy landscape,

Stretches out everywhere: nothing

Snow, footprints, beads of ice clinging

To tree branches the pale moon climbs between

The wood stove is quiet: split wood,

Scraps on the hearth, snow melts on the lawn

Somewhere the sun shines. Peach blossoms

Float on a pond. Another fell just now.

Yesterday bare tree limbs. Today their plumage

White and full -- when will they take flight?

A hard crust of snow covers what we

Remember: grass, dandelions

Morning returns (sky) above the snowy rooftops

blood-orange stain. Sun rises brightly through

A swirling of snowflakes defining the wind

Another red wound bleeds into the sky above

The trees wait for rain. From red to dark grey

The morning sky fills with damp arousal

Life Sentences

Dark morning sky, white silk clouds (whirling) veil a
crescent moon.

Sky is the limitless possible blue, emptiness beyond
breath.

Dogwoods in winter take root in low-hanging clouds;
white blossoms drift.

No sign of sun in days; cold rain drips all morning on
garden Buddha.

Sun not yet risen, meditation gong chimes twice; dog

settles to wait.

Coldest night of the year; no woman to share my bed

(heartbeats), heart beats slow.

Last night's fire hissed cold; kindled, coiled embers burst:

hooves of a galloping horse!

Champagne bottles pop; New Year's fireworks echo

popcorn in the pan.

Snow in the tree limbs, drifts cover the stove lengths --

ashes and ice melt.

Snow slides off my roof, drips echo down the drainpipe:

cold ashes, warm rain.

A small patch of snow under the bush where my dog

pees: remnant of a cloud.

The air teems with life; I breathe in oceans of fish, cough

up shipwrecks.

Fine mist surrounds me; trees blur and wave in the wind:

where have the birds gone?

After two months home, younger son packed up to go:

neither there nor here.

Twigs in the lamplight glisten in damp morning air,

lingering sadness.

Spider startles me almost invisible when I clap my hands:

moist!

You are leaving me; I open my mouth to speak: wind leaf branch rain.

Contemplation

You think about death

And decide it is a long way off

Like that final mortgage payment on the summer house

Or world peace

You set off for California once

Hitchhiking to the Haight --

A good idea at the time, no doubt --

But you never got there it was so far off

You turned back in Missouri

Death is even farther off

Like a planet beyond Pluto

Or justice for all

No point in even thinking about it

If death wants you

Won't it come knocking

On a winter evening when the snow

Swirls ominously

When the wind laughs sardonically

When all the distances close in

The Absence His Presence Implied

When he walked in the room

Everyone was thinking where has he been

Avoiding us maybe

Traveling to exotic locales

Working on his scrabble chops

Oh you didn't hear

She left him

Cancer I heard it was

Lost his job or maybe got a new one

As though a dozen quills suddenly got wet

Scratched across the parchment

A reflex

We couldn't help our jerking knees

The silence was deafening

So we nailed up sound proofing

Turned to one another and resumed

Our mindless chatter

Something Else

It was an ordinary day, except for one thing.

It was a day when the wheel turned the other way.

Like, you could say it had been clockwise until then,

rolling along predictably in the well-worn grooves of

consistent practice.

If you did a thing over and over, it must be okay because

that's the way it went. Uh uh!

This was a change in energy. Polar.

If you are wearing a Hawaiian shirt, I'd recommend you

pick up some quilted technical fabrics rated for 30 below.

If you spend your life smiling at the trivial peccadilloes of your fellows, get used to weeping at their misfortunes.

It was like black was white, front was back, wrong was right.

And it was such a simple thing.

So that's what happened.

It was something else.

You can deal with the experience yourself.

I'm not going to help you.

Life Lessons

for the ghost of John Berryman

I, too, dislike it, heartily,

and I was hoping to avoid

this assignment, the anxiety of influence, the hallowed

canon of world literature –

with one possible exception –

the weight of history, the horoscope I got today,

the Tao of Physics, Robert's Rules of Order,

the preempting of real human interaction by Facebook

and Twitter,

the absence of truth in packaging,

the American Dream going over the falls,

the death of the novel, again,

the nervous consensus among poets that poetry is no longer relevant,

the corruption of judges and sports referees, especially the latter,

the reward for all that hard work being paid in devalued currency,

the way you don't have sex anymore, once you've figured out what you really want,

the illusion that you actually understand anything.

No, it's just possible that

Jabberwocky is the one true cross, and the holy foreskin
is a forgery,

Mohammed's mountain never moved an inch,

Nostradamus was a sloppy poet who you could read any
way you want,

and there never was a Buddha until someone started
making statues profitably.

I don't know about you, but I'm not waiting at this bus
stop anymore.

I just remembered I left the stove on at home.

There's pan of water with an imaginary frog in it, reaching

a boil.

Silence

In the end when he can no longer

Keep his vow of silence

A single wu pops out

As though he were responding

To a koan without answer

He has given up fearing to damage

The world by speaking

Or writing that he knows

There is no truth in packaging

Even cereal boxes lie

Protecting the enormous wealth

Of the gnomes

Pulling puppet strings

From their perch up in the cloud

Making the little people dance

Around the bonfire

Fed by their few belongings

And so life goes on and on

Concealing evil as we aspire

To the good like Sysifus

This is the basis of all comedy

Our failed attempts

To be better than butter

And of course tragedy

We cannot neglect

To water that bamboo tree

Occurs whenever we believe

That we *are* butter

Or worse, better than we are

He knows only silence is

A refuge he's forsaken

He cannot return

Through the palace of worldly

Excess to innocence

Though once he knew another way

Through the portal of ukiyo

Living only for the moment

Floating carefree

A gourd in the river currents

Where moon, snow, blossoms

Of the flowering cherry tree,

Loosened his robes

In his hand a sake cup

In his mouth a song

Now at his feet fallen maple leaves

The Hostage Trade

This morning tearing purple

kale off the stalk

to soak in the lettuce spinner

Their muted hues

purple, green and red

Veiny swatches of ancient madder

Fractile edges --

I thought of all the dead

Unwilling to trade

Meat for healing greens like

Some pompous politician

In a hostage crisis

Refusing to negotiate

With bearded vegans

Let them eat their words

For a week, he confided

To a Monsanto flack --

See if we can't get them

Groveling for a juicy burger

Made from tortured cows

Fed only GMOs

They Think They Know You

You volunteer at a homeless shelter and take lots

Of cans to the kettles and boxes, too

Otherwise, you vote Republican It's a family thing

Yes, the politicians act so sure and so unbending

You don't even know if what you believe

If it could be put into words that made sense

It's mostly feelings you've had since you were small

Fairness and virtue and just being nice

Do figure into it though not as independent variables

The calculus of your politics is not easy to compute

Maybe you're not a Republican after all

You just voted that way because everyone said

The Democrats just want to give it all away

To those poor and homeless and we know the truth

They're just plain lazy drink too much and have

Unprotected sex so they can collect more for babies

It's hard work that made this country great

That and lots of guns and bombs

Isn't that what they said something like it anyway

You think about the slaughter of war, and it's ugly

You think about babies crying out for food and for love

You think about the doors locked by prejudice

And wish you had the key to unlock just one

Just one cruelty you could eradicate forever

Just one greed

There is no doubting

The poshlust of human beings, yet we praise them

As though to raise them up

They Don't Eat Vegetables, Do They?

One of the problems with AA

You don't see it mentioned a lot in the press

Is a lack of faith

In lesser powers, that is, like Doritos, Snickers

And bottled water

Do you remember drinking fountains?

How about the ones that had signs over them?

No gay men or women

No transsexuals

No blacks or mulattos

Of course different words were used

No women with small breasts or attitude

According to the OED

Buxom means compliant

I haven't found that to be the case

Could give you examples

No men who imitate Ricardo Montalban

Sam Elliott, Peter Coyote

or the most interesting man in the world

And here's why

Nobody knows the answer

To the 64 thousand dollar questions

Without whispered answers

Everyone wants to be the pebble in the pond

That creates the ripple for change

And they all know what makes them nervous

Even if they don't know why

You don't want to walk into a party

Without a gift for the hostess

Or a covered casserole dish

Something that needs the oven right away

Like a suicide

You want the kitchen to be at your disposal

I'm not talking garbage

I'm talking knifes

Whole butcher's blocks of them

Knives to slice the meat from bone

Knives to remove a fish's rib cage

Serrated spoons to lift away the organs

Not that AA has anything at all to do with organs

Willing or weak we all howl at the full moon

We all wonder what it took from us

When it was here last week

And when it will return

Was it sanity? Was it fertility? Was it an election?

That's where the deaths of innocent children

Trump all causes all nationalities all faiths

Even Rush Limbaugh has to admit he loves children

Christian children, white Christian children particularly

And mostly boys

Women pose too many challenges

For an unrepentant drug addict to cope with

So never mind Rush

He'll get his, already has

Let's focus on us and why nobody eats vegetables

The simple truth is

Eating meat is more a unifying practice than the national
anthem

Most of us cringe at the rockets red glare

And if the words weren't bad enough, it's so darn hard to
sing

Just ask Oscar Meyer if you want a catchy tune

You know I love it in a movie when somebody

Says I think we're done here

And they haven't even scratched the surface

The Most Secret Lie

Once we are across the river

We leave the boat behind

There are exceptions notably

I've seen the best minds of my generation

Carrying on their bony backs

The skiffs they came in with

Others simply camped at the river's edge

Turned their boats over

Raised them up on stilts and lived there

Like a memory

Of winning that state of bliss

The high school football championship

They inhabit their trophies

Crawl by on all fours

Dream at night of leaving it all behind

Like turtle soup or escargot or

Siddhartha sneaking out of the palace

After everyone's asleep or drunk

Homeless under a new moon

And a ficus tree

Yet once free of desire

We must also break free

Of any desire to be free

Not only of desire

Free of the boat on our backs

Shame too

As in isn't it a shame?

Billy was such a cute little boy

Promising young man

Fine upstanding father tribal elder mensch

That plunge from the precipice

Into a quarry filled with

Rusted automobile parts, blown tires

discarded guns and knives

We all watched him dive

Headfirst into waters far too shallow

For survival

Yet we were too callow to stop him

Or the fall he took

Into a disgrace thick enough to stir

With a whisk yet thinner

Than a close shave with a straight razor

His tonsure neatly trimmed

A sporty set of chin whiskers

Soul patch and goatee

Enthralling his distaff flock with wit

He whispered to those gathered about him

The most secret lie

As plastic flowers decked the altar

Fading under the gaze of those

Who had left their boats behind

He said leaving his feet

There is more to life than life and also less

Seasons

1

gate swings

bolt clangs

hasty departure

2

plastic bag

caught in a branch

leafless tree

3 snow crust the dog melts diamonds on his tongue

4

die is forever

yesterday

in the green sod

When Stuff Is Not Enough

I took a picture of a peacock feeding on the lawn

In the Dominican Republic a while back

Self-portrait you could say as in

Aren't all the things we see

Mere projections of ourselves

No two ways about it said Krishnamurti

Yet I'd gone to that resort to find myself

Not bring myself along

I hadn't gone to nearby Haiti

To shoot Uncle Gunnysack

Or a voodoo priestess in top hat and whiteface

I hadn't gone to the Yucatan to ponder

Mayan hieroglyphs

I hadn't gone to Cuba to drink rum

Maybe I should have stayed at home

Shoveling snow in February

Walking my dog in the blue dark of early morning

Crumpling newspaper to stoke my wood stove

A news feature might have caught my eye

Instead of a peacock with ragged tail feathers

A story about an eminent psychologist

Researching happiness in twelve languages

He'd made his journey to find

Not himself but what made people smile inside

Was it ever possible he wondered

To be happy and cause no pain to others

Or is all mirth *schadenfreude*

I remember hearing Nancy Aronie say

The best laughter is at your own expense

Saving up embarrassment and shame

Like pennies in the belly of a pig

One day will oink dividends of joy

What sends a man around the world

In search of happiness

A child holds in the palm of her tiny hand

And her grown up parents squander

Don't you sometimes wonder

What's enough

Just the right amount of stuff and time

To make the most of it or leastwise

Share with someone else

I took a picture of a peacock feeding on the lawn

When I was alone

There was no you no Catholic no Jew

No French nor Russian Republican

No colors on a map no tattoo

No other vegetarians I could see but me

So I ate fish and coconuts

Meditating reading walking the beach

Remembering to smile

I whiled away the days doing little else

It was enough

I forgot myself I forgot my stuff

ACKNOWLEDGEMENTS

Some of these poems I have performed at The Vineyard Playhouse, Pathways, and at the West Tisbury and Vineyard Haven libraries. Thanks to all who have opened their minds to these poems.

BIOGRAPHY

Michael G. West, a graduate of Williams College and the Johns Hopkins Writing Seminars, has published poems in chapbooks, little magazines and online journals. In addition to poems, he has published five novels, two in the Tommy Shakespear Mystery Thriller and three in the Martha's Vineyard EcoThriller series. He has worked as a dishwasher, short-order cook, housepainter, shingler, sheetrock taper, private tutor, taxi driver, college professor, freelance book editor, computer programmer, industry analyst and strategy consultant in several countries and on both coasts, north and south, in the U.S. He currently lives year round on Martha's Vineyard, an island off Cape Cod, Massachusetts. He has two sons, several ex-wives and a dog named Leo.

Made in the USA
Middletown, DE
11 January 2017